ARDUINO PROGRAMMING

A COMPLETE BEGINNERS' GUIDE ON LEARNING TO ENGINEER AND PROGRAM ARDUINO

Jason Hamilton

© **Copyright 2020 by Jason Hamilton**

All rights reserved.

The follow eBook is reproduced below with the goal of providing information that is as accurate and reliable as possible. Regardless, purchasing this eBook can be seen as consent to the fact that both the publisher and the author of this book are in no way experts on the topics discussed within and that any recommendations or suggestions that are made herein are for entertainment purposes only. Professionals should be consulted as needed prior to undertaking any of the action endorsed herein.

This declaration is deemed fair and valid by both the American Bar Association and the Committee of Publishers Association and is legally binding throughout the United States.

Furthermore, the transmission, duplication or reproduction of any of the following work including specific information will be considered an illegal act irrespective of if it is done electronically or in print. This extends to creating a secondary or tertiary copy of the work or a recorded copy and is only allowed with express written consent from the Publisher. All additional right reserved.

The information in the following pages is broadly considered to be a truthful and accurate account of facts and as such any inattention, use or misuse of the information in question by the reader will render any resulting actions solely under their purview. There are no scenarios in which the publisher or the original author of this work can be in any fashion deemed liable for any hardship or damages that may befall them after undertaking information described herein.

Table of Contents

Introduction 4

Chapter One: Introducing Arduino 5

Chapter Two: Arduino IDE 13

Chapter Three: Arduino Boards... 22

Chapter Four: Recent Information on Arduino Usage......... 35

Chapter Five: Arduino Coding Principles............................. 43

Chapter Six: Arduino C Data.. 50

Chapter Seven: 10 Great Beginners' Projects with Arduino..61

Chapter Eight: Fixing Common Arduino Troubleshooting Problems... 98

Final Words 105

Introduction

Are you looking for a detailed and precise book on learning Arduino?

Let's cut the loose ends of wiring/programming and learn what you need to know.

An up to date practise of Arduino is found throughout this novella. You will Explore the core requirements of Arduino. Learn the history behind it and learn how to use Arduino boards in order to make your own projects. Jason Hamilton walks you through the basics of Arduino, he explains the electrical engineering, human-computer interactions and the complex data programming codes that are required. If you get stuck, we have you covered in chapter eight.

Whether you are a beginner or an intermediate with Arduino. Jason demonstrates how to navigate your way around Arduino Programming and boards with the use of detailed knowledge and pictures. Delve into the depths of this novella and keep it handy as you are building/ programming your Arduino project. There are many codes and sequences you will need to follow in order to complete your project. So, this will essentially become your handbook.

This book offers an in-depth introduction into using Arduino and gives a step by step guide on what to look for and what to do in building 10 beginner projects that will make you ecstatic about.

Well what are you waiting for?... Start your journey to your new beloved hobby. Purchase this book and you'll obtain the skills and knowledge required to build and program your very own micro controlled prototypes or projects!

Chapter One: Introducing Arduino

What is Arduino?

Arduino is an electronics system used to create interactive objects for human comfort. It is a mini computer with hardware and software components that is capable of working online or offline. Its software component, the Arduino IDE, can be downloaded from the Arduino website, and it comes with several easy-to-use features and capabilities. The Arduino IDE (Integrated Development Environment) is used to initiate commands for the hardware component, development board, and runs fine on all operating systems—a situation that made it a cross-platform microcontroller.

The development board is a programmable, ready-to-use circuit designed to take coded instructions from the IDE and affect prompt execution. In executing required actions, the Arduino board works closely with the connected sensors and input devices, being tools used to control electronics and build interactive objects. The board uses these tools to read inputs, control outputs, and execute desired actions.

Arduino is an open-source programmable platform, meaning that it enjoys program flexibility. Its programs move to the Arduino development board via a USB cable. This board is capable of performing several tasks in the physical world. It can sense and control objects, respond to sensors and inputs, and handle all sorts of outputs, including LEDs and displays. Its ability to create interactive hardware projects and breathe life into amazing project imaginations have made it the popular choice for people who work in both professional and hobby industries. Written-and-run IDE programs are commonly known as sketch instruction codes that the Arduino board uses to build hardware projects. Programming languages are used to code instructions for the board to create interactive objects.

Arduino—being a microcontroller—comes with an integrated circuit that records coded instructions and has all the required peripherals to connect input and output components of regular personal computers. Its serial communication peripheral means that Arduino can work well on personal computers. Arduino comes with 14 digital pins numbered from 0 to 13. These pins can run both input and output operations, depending on their setup. They are designed to read voltage as high or low when set as inputs but will go a step further to apply voltage when set as outputs. These pins aid serial communication between Arduino and other electronics, especially when new instruction codes are uploaded. Digital badges are to be used only for serial interface, or they may soon run out.

Like many other microcontrollers, Arduino works mainly via its input and exit interfaces. The input interface can be connected directly to the computer through ports or linked through its peripherals and can aid the transfer of data from the computer to the Arduino board, where it would be processed. The exit interface picks up the job once the data gets to the Arduino board.

Why Arduino?

Already, Arduino has become the popular choice of many people in the professional and hobby industries, and its acceptance is growing daily thanks to fantastic hardware projects that people build with it. The pertinent question on the lips of many people is: what makes Arduino unique or different from other microcontrollers? In answering this question, a co-founder of Arduino Massimo Banzi highlighted the reasons why Arduino has remained the choice of many (Louis, 2016):

1. **Active User Community:** Arduino offers a free interactive community for its teeming users to share ideas, experiences, and get their everyday troubleshooting issues resolved. Users of similar products now have the opportunity to share thoughts via posted conversations.

2. **User-friendly Features:** Arduino is a user-friendly microcontroller capable of creating hardware devices that could interact with the environment through sensors and actuators. Its trouble-free features have made it the go-to microcontroller for creating amazing hardware projects.

3. **Inexpensive Hardware:** Arduino is an open-source, programmable microcontroller. Users do not have to purchase hardware designs or software; only the board or needed parts need to be purchased. You can download the hardware designs and the software online free of charge from www.arduino.cc, the official website of Arduino.

4. **The versatility of the Arduino Board:** One thing that makes the Arduino board unique is its versatility. It is easy to use and usable everywhere. It can function as a programmer, and its USB cable is strong enough to moderate its power requirements.

5. **Cross-platform:** Users love Arduino because it can work on popular platforms such as Mac, Linux, and Windows operating systems, unlike some

microcontrollers that only run on Windows. The Arduino user community is also always growing.

Regular Users of Arduino

Arduino was a fast prototyping tool for students who never had electronics and programming backgrounds. People had hardly been using it before new needs and challenges began to emerge. Still, Arduino went ahead to adjust its mode of operations in a desperate bid to address emerging needs. Users too began to create hardware projects that were capable of meeting public needs, but this would not have been possible if Arduino boards and software were not open source. What was initially intended for students has now been used to create fantastic hardware objects in all areas of human endeavour. Regular users of Arduino include teachers, students, electricians, designers, architects, musicians, and artists.

Teachers and students use it to design low-cost, scientific teaching aids and test physics and chemistry principles. It is also a go-to centre for those who have a passion for programming and robotics.

Electricians often use it for prototyping their products and showcasing their ideas. They can also use it to build amazing projects like solar streetlight, home automation, industrial appliance control, cable fault detection, and obstacle avoidance.

Designers and architects use Arduino to design cell walls, dynamic environments, and other interactive prototypes, while musicians and artists can experiment with their new musical instruments on Arduino.

Arduino is a user-friendly learning tool that can be used by everyone.

History of Arduino

The need to design a fast prototyping tool for students who never had electronics and programming backgrounds led to the production of Arduino in 2005 at the Interactive Design Institute in Ivrea, Italy. Right there in a classroom, Hernando Barragan, a Colombian student of the institute, postulated a hardware thesis for the production of a wiring design. His title then was *Arduino—La rivoluzione dell'open hardware*, which can be translated to *Arduino—'The Revolution of Open Hardware'*. Massimo Banzi and David Cuartielles adopted this thesis to design a pocket-friendly programmable device now known as Arduino.

Banzi was a software architect before the institute recruited him as an associate professor in 2002 to teach students new ways of doing physical computing. He could not showcase his amazing ideas because he had issues of budget and limited class time. His inability to work on his amazing ideas made him use BASIC Stamp—the popular microcontroller of the time. Banzi had issues with the Stamp because its computing power was too small to run some of his students' conceptualized projects, and it was costly. He had a viable interest in a microcontroller that would be compatible with Macintosh computers because designers hardly use other computers at the institute.

Meanwhile, *Processing*—a designed user-friendly programming language—had caught the attention of Banzi. The programming language was so good that even amateur programmers could use it easily to develop beautiful and complex visualizations. Banzi planned to create a similar program, but one that could code a microcontroller, not just graphics displayed on a screen. It was Hernando who took the first step to create something similar to processing. His design—a user-friendly and ready-to-use circuit board—became known as *Wiring* and was a promising project of the time; however, Banzi had bigger dreams. He wanted a microcontroller that was far cheaper and easier to use, a feat he achieved in 2005 when he successfully built the prototype board.

So, working on the wiring thesis of Hernando Barragan, Massimo Banzi, and David Cuartielles created Arduino to aid the creation of fantastic hardware design projects. David Mellis later developed the Arduino software before Gianluca Martino and Tom Igoe joined the project. Already considered as the founders of Arduino, the five developers worked to produce an easy-to-use and less expensive microcontroller that could connect relays, motors, sensors, and other devices.

Advantages of Arduino

Consider some of the advantages of using Arduino below:

1. **Ready for Use:** Arduino board is a user-friendly, ready-to-use microcontroller with a complete package of LED and connection headers. It also comes with a burner, oscillator, serial communication interface, and a 5V regulator. Anyone who intends to purchase the Board needs not worry about how to program or install it. Connect the board via your computer's USB port, and you are good to go.

2. **Effortless Functions:** Coding is straightforward on Arduino because it runs a few user-friendly functions. It's simple but effective built-in features mean that no time is wasted when creating exciting projects. Also, users need not worry about unit conversions during debugging because the system can run automatic translations. All the user needs to do is concentrate on

significant areas of the projects—not possible side issues.

3. **Large Community:** The internet has many forums where engineers, hobbyists, students, and other professionals can share stories of projects executed with Arduino. These forums show that Arduino has a vast community of users where people can find solutions to their troubleshooting issues. Visit the official website of Arduino to access their product information and functions.

4. **Access to Online Information:** Loads of helpful content is available online for people who are stuck in the middle of their projects. The Arduino website has answers to users' queries about the product. Still, additional help could be obtained from online communities and social media groups, where project experts would share their Arduino experiences.

5. **Inexpensive:** Arduino boards are more pocket-friendly than other microcontrollers in the market.

6. **Cross-platform:** Arduino software is not like other microcontroller IDEs, which only run on Windows. It runs perfectly on Linux, Macintosh, and Windows operating systems.

Disadvantages of Arduino

Past users of Arduino have raised specific issues about the product. Issues raised include:

1. **Structure:** Arduino's prominent structure is not ideal for every project. It is excellent for anyone who is working on big projects because of its big-sized PCBs, but you need to reduce the structure to accommodate

smaller projects. It shouldn't pose a serious challenge to people working on ATmega8 or any small microcontroller because they could get the PCB cut to the size of the projects, they are handling.

2. **Cost:** Arduino boards may be more pocket-friendly than other microcontrollers in the market, but its value to run a few similar small projects at a time could be hard to bear. For example, anyone who is planning to build three or four smart energy meters apart but are connected with different loads would need to purchase a separate processor for each meter.

3. **Ease-of-usage:** This might sound strange, but the ease-of-usage features of Arduino hardware and software remain its biggest weakness. Arduino makes everything simple for people to the extent that nobody is ready to learn the complex, intelligent circuit processes involved in the creation of significant interactive objects. So, most people stick to the basic boards instead of the better-quality ones.

Chapter Two: Arduino IDE

What is the Arduino IDE?

Arduino Integrated Development Environment—an open-source and easy-to-use software—is compatible with popular operating systems such as Windows, Linux, Apple, and Macintosh. It is mainly used for programming codes, compiling codes, debugging codes, accepting information, and giving commands to the Arduino board. The two distinct areas of the IDE are *Editor* and *Compiler*. Although the *Editor* is mainly used to write code—also known as sketch—the *Compiler* compiles and uploads the sketch to the Arduino board. You can use the C and C++ languages to write code on the software. The software page on the Arduino website would support both online and offline coding. Users with reliable internet connections can use the online IDE to program their codes and save their sketches in the cloud. The highlight of this online IDE is that users will have access to the up-to-date version of the software with necessary feature updates. Offline users would have to download the recent release of the IDE from www.arduino.co/en/main/software.

Users should download the software from the Arduino website displayed above because that is where they can see original and up-to-date versions of the IDE. However, users should consider the release of the IDE they intend to download carefully to be sure it's compatible with their operating system. Computers running on Windows should be upgraded to Windows 8.1 or Windows 10 because the software will not work on Windows 7 and older Windows versions. Arduino IDE has these three key sections.

1. **Menu Bar:** The menu bar lies at the top of the software. A click on this bar will show five options.

   - **File:** Select this option if you want to program code in a new window or open one already stored on your system.

   - **Edit:** Here, you can modify the font used for the coding exercise and copy and paste it as you want.

   - **Sketch:** Use this to compile and program the code.

   - **Tools:** Use this to test your projects and burn it to the microcontroller in the Arduino board.

   - **Help:** Tap this if you need help with running your projects via the software.

Right there under the Menu tab are six buttons. Users need to understand these buttons and how to use them.

- **Check mark:** Mark is a circular button used for code verification. Do click the button once you finish writing your code.

- **Arrow key:** Use the arrow key to upload or transfer the written code to the board.

- **Dotted paper:** Use this paper to create a new file.

- **Upward arrow:** Use this arrow only when you want to open an existing project.

- **Downward arrow:** Click the arrow when you want to save your code.

- **Serial Monitor:** The serial monitor lies at the top-right-hand corner of the Arduino IDE. Use it to debug written codes, send and receive serial data.

2. **Text Editor:** Just below the Menu bar, you will see the screen for the text editor, where you can program your code.

3. **Output Pane:** The output pane occupies the bottom part of the text editor, and it shows the compilation status of the code you are running, the memory it has used, and errors already encountered. You must fix these errors before you can send your code to the board.

Digital pins on the Arduino board can run input and output functions, but this depends on the commands you give them via the software. Although digital read controls make Arduino pins run input functions, digital write commands will instruct these pins to run output functions. Use the commands as they appear here because they are case sensitive.

Arduino C—like the regular C languages used in programming other system microcontrollers—works fine, but other amazing libraries could execute specific functions on the Arduino board. Click the sketch button to add these extra functions. Click the Menu bar >Include Library >Add the libraries you want. It is as simple as that.

The Arduino IDE comes with most of these libraries, but there are other external sources where you can download them too. However, do make sure that you select your board, ports, and operating system correctly before you get your code uploaded, and these steps will aid your progress.

1. Click Menu bar >Tools >Board >Select your board
2. Click Windows Device Manager

3. Select Ports >USB serial device >Click Verify

4. Click Upload

New Arduino boards can do an automatic reset once the written codes are uploaded, but users of old versions may need to punch the reset button on their boards to do it manually. The TX and RX LEDs on the board will blink to show that the program execution was successful. There is a built-in bootloader in the Arduino board where one can burn or upload the codes.

How to Program Arduino IDE

Coding on the Arduino software is an *if-then* logic, and its four main structural blocks aid it. Take a look at the blocks and unique functions they are used to perform.

1. **Setup:** Right there in the setup section of the Arduino sketch lies the setup () function. Use it to prompt the start of a sketch, variables, pin modes, and libraries. It handles sensor calibration and other tasks that are performed one at a time. The function can only run when the Arduino board goes through a reset. It also shows the input and output interactions of the board with the serial monitor.

2. **Loop:** The input, which is the first part of the logic (if)—sets the tone of action for the loop () function— Loop is used to aid the smooth operation of the Arduino circuit on the computer. The loop ensures that programs run consecutively, thereby giving the system ample opportunity to respond to each application.

3. **Manipulative Data:** Manipulative data aids the transformation of data to forms that are suitable for calculations. For example, the 0-1023 reading of the

Analog Read () command can cover the range of 0-255, which is ideal for the Pulse-width modulation (PWM).

4. **Output:** Output is the second part (then) of the logic, and it centres mainly on the manipulative data arrived at by the system.

Program your Arduino IDE with these simple steps.

1. Install your Arduino IDE
2. Connect the Arduino board to your computer via its USB port
3. Launch IDE and open preloaded sketch
4. Click Menu bar >Tools >Board >Select your board
5. Click Windows Device Manager >Ports >USB serial device >Verify >Upload
6. Upload a new sketch and disconnect the board.

How to Install Arduino IDE

The latest versions of Arduino IDE come in Installer (.exe) or Zip forms. Still, users should use the Installer because it would have everything they need to run the software successfully, including the drivers. People who intend to use the Zip package would have to get the drivers installed manually. Download the Arduino IDE from www.arduino.cc, which is the official website of Arduino, and continue the installation process by following these simple steps.

1. Install the driver
2. Agree to the Licensing Agreement

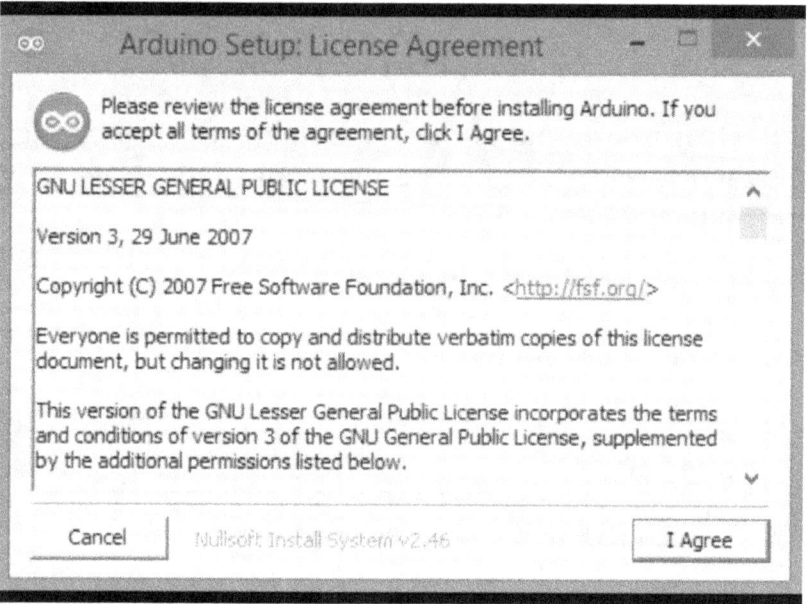

3. Install Desired Components and click Next

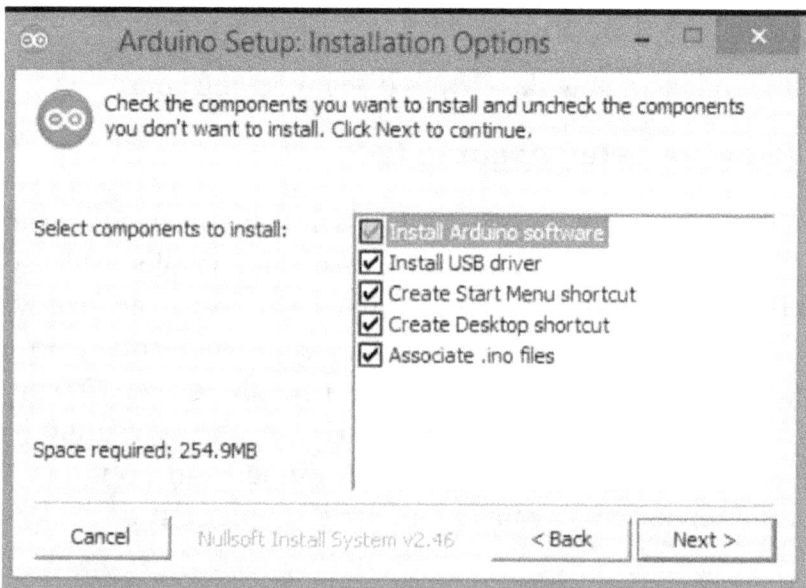

4. Select the Directory Folder to install the program, and tap Install

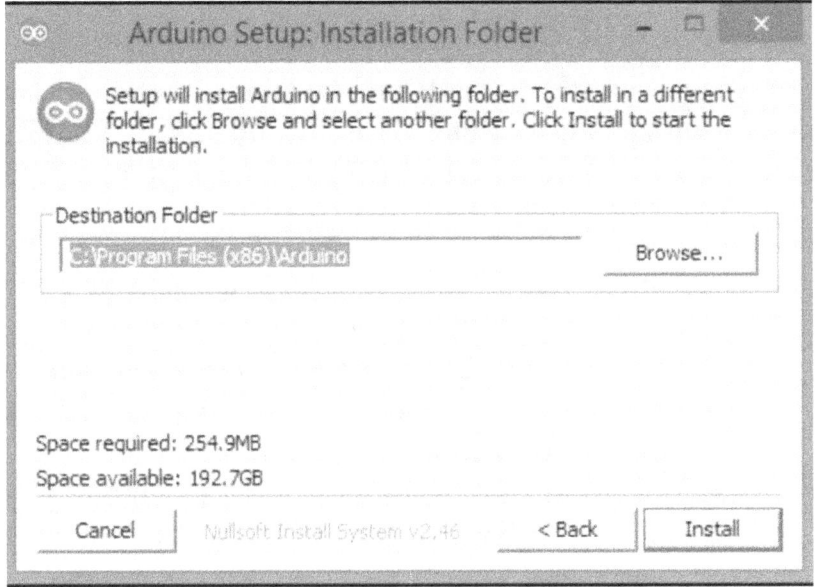

5. Allow the installation to complete, then click Close

6. Click the shortcut on your Desktop to open the software

7. Move along with the installation process by following these simple steps.

Having the Arduino software installed is not the only thing required to start coding. The already-installed software needs to be configured correctly to work with the type of Arduino board one intends to work with, especially for those who use more than one kind of Arduino board on their computer. Such people should configure their Arduino IDE with these simple steps.

Click Menu tab >Tools >Select the installed board >Windows Device Manager >Ports >USB serial device >Verify.

Uses of Arduino IDE

Anyone can use the software to build unusual physical objects from all walks of life. Here are some of the industry-based projects that the Arduino IDE has been used to execute.

1. **Sensors Projects:** Arduino IDE has been used to create many sensors projects such as a wooden knocking calculator, smartwatch prototype, and automatic pet watering system. The wooden calculator can run mathematical operations while the smartwatch prototype functions as a regular smartphone. The watering system can balance the water in a tub by filling the container with water when the water level is low.

2. **ICT Projects:** Arduino software has been used to execute a good number of ICT projects. Some of these projects are mind-controlled robots, gaming robots, and robotic fish. The mind-controlled robot is controlled by the electrical signals produced by the human brain. The amount of focus directed to the robot would determine its pace of movement. The gaming robot is another interactive robot designed to play games with humans, especially when people mimic its actions. The robotic fish can swim like any normal fish and may be used to explore the sea via unique sea cameras.

3. **Wireless Projects:** Several wireless projects such as home automation and power meters have been successfully built with the Arduino software. Home appliances can be controlled with a home automation Wi-Fi device while a power meter can get the range of energy consumed in homes. Such projects bring no small comfort to the apartments.

4. **Security Projects:** Physical interactive objects such as home security systems or night security alarms can be built with the Arduino software to secure homes and offices from unauthorized third parties. The home security system can be used to secure the properties in the house and prevent unauthorized persons from gaining entrance into the guaranteed space. By contrast, the night security alarm is designed to provide all-night security against theft and theft attempts.

Exploring the Arduino Software

The Arduino IDE is a user-friendly software that comes with different albeit easy-to-use menus, where users can view amazing program examples. The Examples menu, for example, can offer insight on how one can begin Arduino projects without being subjected to a lot of research. Feel free to explore these programs. Parts of the code can be changed to see the effect that will be created, since it is an excellent way of learning the basics of programming; however, these examples cannot make anyone an overnight expert at programming. It pays when one codes their own program from scratch. Learning programming will become more comfortable when one picks a precious book on Arduino projects. A good book should go through the project examples and replicate the samples in real life.

Chapter Three: Arduino Boards

What are Arduino Boards?

Arduino boards are ready-to-use, open-source, programmable circuits designed to read information and initiate commands. Being microcontrollers, the Arduino boards work with sensors and input devices and can be used to relate with LEDs, motors, displays, and other physical interactive objects. They are tools people use to control electronics and create hardware devices that can interact with the environment.

Sensors and shields can aid the interaction of the Arduino board with its physical environment. Several sensors can be added to the board, but users need to consider the objects they intend to build first. Why? Each sensor has a unique purpose. Conventional sensors for hardware projects include (but are not limited to) a light sensor, humidity and temperature sensor, sound detecting sensor, proximity sensor, and acceleration sensor.

Shields, on the other hand, are designed circuit boards that could be plugged to the headers of the Arduino. These shields help extend the functionalities and capabilities of Arduino boards and are sensor' look-alikes. Shields can be used to add desired functions such as GPS, Bluetooth, LCD, MP3, Ethernet, and Wi-Fi to the Arduino board, although each shield has a particular role to play. For example, the Arduino shield used to connect the board to the internet is quite different from the one used to add functions like GPS or Bluetooth. These shields can be downloaded online because they are all open-source tools. While several companies sell Arduino boards, users should purchase their boards from www.arduino.cc, the official website of the Arduino company.

Components of Arduino Board

The Arduino board consists of hardware and software components. We will only discuss the hardware component here because the Arduino IDE—the software component of Arduino—has been discussed extensively in the last chapter. Feel free to return back to it if you need a refresher. Here are the main hardware parts of the Arduino board.

1. **Microcontroller:** This is the soul of the board. It helps the board receive information from users and transmit command signals to devices that are connected to the Arduino board.

2. **External Power Supply:** This does not only power the Arduino board but also ensures the voltage is regulated between 9 and 12 volts. The power supply should be selected carefully because it can damage the board if it produces over 20 volts.

3. **USB Plug:** The USB plug has many essential functions for the board. It can be used to burn a sketch via the USB cable or power the board in the absence of the external power supply.

4. **Pins:** Arduino boards come with analog, digital, AREF, PWM, 5V, 3.3V, and GND pins. These pins enable users to plug wires to the Arduino board and perform different functions.

GND stands for *Ground*. The board comes with a few GND pins, and they help ground circuits. 5V and 3.3V pins only supply volts of power to the board. Just like their names, the board gets 5 volts from the 5V pin and 3.3 volts from the other pin. Analog pins are labelled from A0 to A5 and are designed to read analog signals. Analog pins vary in numbers in Arduino boards, but they perform similar functions. Digital pins are labelled from 0 to 13, and they sit across the analog pins. They run digital input and output functions for users. PWM stands for Pulse-Width Modulation. PWM pins are individual, digital pins that are used to control analog output. AREF is nothing but Analog Reference. It is always idle unless the external reference voltage needs to be set.

5. **Reset Button:** Press the reset button when you want to reset the board or restart a code on the Arduino. Use it to test the functionality of codes multiple times, especially when those codes often fail to repeat.

6. **Power LED Indicator:** Each Arduino board has a tiny power LED indicator that lights up the board when it has been plugged into a power source.

7. **Main IC:** Also known as the brain of the circuit, the main IC is black and comes with metal legs, but it depends on the type of board one is using. Users need to know their board and IC type, or they may have issues uploading new programs via their Arduino software.

8. **Voltage Regulator:** Users do not have to interact with the voltage regulator. It is designed to regulate the voltage that gets into the board.

Popular Arduino Boards

1. **Arduino Uno:** This easy-to-use board appears to be the most popular Arduino board in the market, especially for beginners. It has a standard USB, which

can be used for programming and power, few female headers, a power input connector, six analog input ports, 14 digital pins for input and output operations, and one hardware serial port.

2. **Arduino Nano:** This board is not as big as the Arduino Uno, but it has the necessary features of a standard Arduino board. It comes with one hardware serial port, 14 digital pins for input and output operations, eight analog input ports, few male headers, and a mini USB, which helps power the Board and run effortless programming.

3. **Arduino Mini:** Arduino Mini remains the smallest of all Arduino boards, and it is used mainly for small projects. It comes with a few male headers, 14 digital ports for input and output operations, and eight analog input ports. Only four of these eight analog ports are connected to the male headers.

4. **Arduino Mega:** This board comprises four serial ports, 54 digital pins for input and output operations, 16 analog input ports, a power input connector, few female headers, and a normal-sized USB for power and programming. Arduino Mega is the most giant, ready-to-use Arduino board in the market.

Programming Arduino Board via a USB

It is quite easy to program a sketch sample to the Arduino board by following these steps.

1. Connect your Arduino board to a computer

2. Click on Menu tab >Tools >Board

3. Select Board, choose the Arduino board you are using, and click Verify.

4. Go back to Menu Tab and click Tools >Serial port >Programmer >AVRISP mkii >Serial port >Choose the right port

5. Click on File and Upload

Here is another way to do it through the 'USB asp'

1. Load the sketch to upload >Click Tools >Programmer >USB asp

2. Go back to Menu tab >Click on Tools >Board >Pick the board you are using >Select File >Upload using Programmer

Types of Arduino Boards

Arduino boards come with different capabilities, and they can be used to create fantastic hardware objects. These boards are open-source, and users can modify them as they like. Here are types of Arduino boards that people can use to explore the world of physical interactive creation.

1. **Arduino Uno:** Beginners will surely love this Arduino board because of its easy-to-understand tips on how to use sensors and actuators, along with its rapid prototyping features. Apart from being the most used Arduino board, most online tutorials and instructions for handling physical interactive projects are centred on the Arduino Uno. The board suits the needs of beginners more than other boards in the Arduino family. Arduino Uno comes with 14 digital pins, but six of these pins function as PWM outputs. Also, the board has six analog inputs, a reset button, USB connection, crystal

oscillator, power jack, and ICSP header. The board has everything beginners can hope for in a microcontroller. Either a USB cable or AC-to-DC adapter may be used to connect it to any regular computer.

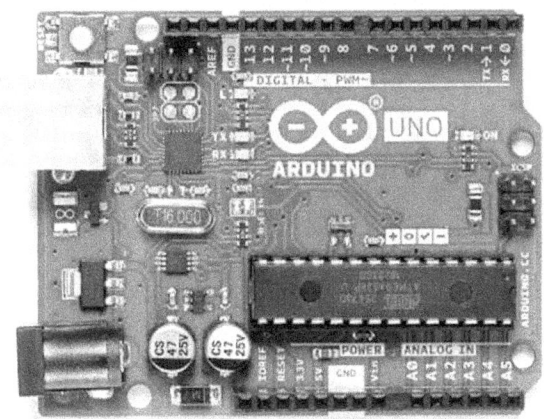

2. **Lilly Pad:** This Arduino board was designed in line with e-textile technology, and it comes with connecting pads and conductive threads for sewing. Like Arduino Uno, the Lily Pad board has pins for input and output operations, power buttons, and sensors boards, and it is meant for people who are working on e-textile and wearable projects. Its power supply requirement is between 2V and 5V, and the board uses its large, pin-out holes for sewing and connection purposes.

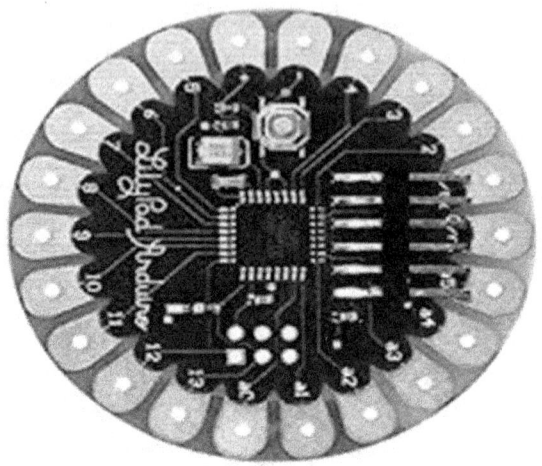

3. **Red Board:** Users of computers running Windows 8 will love this Arduino board because they don't have to modify their security settings before they can use it. They can install the board with a mini-B USB cable through the help of compatible software. Many people love this board because of its flat back and FTDI chips.

4. **Mega:** Two physical differences between the Arduino mega board and Uno are the former's large size and many digital input and output pins. The board comes with a reset button and a power jack, while 14 out of its

54 digital pins run PWM functions. Arduino mega board is mainly designed for projects that require many digital input and output pins. Like the Uno, the Arduino mega board can be powered with a computer-connected USB cable or AC-to-DC adapter.

5. **Leonardo Board:** This was the first Arduino board ever produced, but it has only one microcontroller and built-in USB communication tool. It is cheaper than other boards within the Arduino family, but only a few people use it to build physical, interactive projects. The Leonardo board does not need secondary processors to work, and it can be connected to the computer via a USB cable or AC-to-DC adapter. It will show like a mouse or keyboard when connected to the computer.

6. **Arduino Shields:** Proto, Ethernet, GSM, and wireless shields are variants of pre-built circuit boards that could be connected to compatible Arduino boards to create more functions and capabilities. Arduino shields can be used to control LCD screens and provide wireless and internet connection for other Arduino boards.

Selecting the Right Board

All Arduino boards come with amazing features and can be used to build great hardware projects, but the tips below can help you select the right board for your projects.

1. Beginners in the world of Arduino should consider purchasing the Arduino Uno board because it is straightforward to use. Again, the board is the focal point of most online tutorials building environmental projects.

2. Users who want a cheap board to do small projects should consider buying the Arduino mini board. It works like the Arduino Uno, but its surface-mounted controller IC could be an issue.

3. Anyone who is running a project that requires a lot of wires and 20 pins or more should just go for Arduino Mega. By its design, the board can be used to run big hardware projects.

How to Install Arduino Board Drivers

Users should search for the Arduino IDE designed for their operating systems before attempting to install the board. The appropriate IDE version of every operating system can be downloaded on the Arduino website. Windows operating systems should have no issue installing Arduino board drivers automatically when they are connected to the board, but installation can be done with these simple steps.

1. Plug the board to your computer: Windows will try to get it installed automatically but don't panic if it fails.

2. Click on the Start menu tab >Right-click Computer to pop up a menu >Click Properties

3. Click Device Manager >Arduino board >Select your board type

4. Right-click Arduino board >Click Update Driver Software to prompt a pop-up dialog box

5. Click Browse my computer for driver software >Select the Drivers folder >Click Next

6. Click "Install this driver software" and wait for the installation to complete.

Arduino Mega Server

The Arduino mega server is built on ATmega2560 and useful for creating 3D printers and robotic projects. With 16 analog pins, 54 digital pins, 4 UARTs ports, and a 16-MHz crystal oscillator, the Arduino mega server exceeds other Arduino boards in features and functions. Arduino can be connected to the Internet after it has been configured as a mega server. Here, we will look at how one can set the Arduino mega board to a mega server.

Components Required

- Arduino Ethernet shield
- Ethernet cable to connect network router
- USB cable to power and program Arduino
- SPI compatible micro SD card
- A micro-SD card compatible computer.

Hardware Setup

Plug an Ethernet shield to the Arduino board and connect to the network router to create a mega server. Use the shield to test the SD card.

Having created the Arduino mega server, let us take it a step further by making the server an HTTP web browser that can host a web page. Open the Arduino IDE on your system and locate Sketch. Write this command there to make Arduino and Ethernet shield a web page that can be viewed.

```
void setup ()
{
Ethernet.begin (mac, ip) ;
server.begin () ;
}
void loop ()
{
EthernetClient client = server.available ();
if (client) {
boolean currentLineIsBlank = true;
while (client.connected()) {
if (client.available()) {
char c = client.read();
if (c == '\n' && currentLineIsBlank) {
client.println("HTTP/1.1 200 OK");
client.println("Content-Type: text/html");
client.println("Connection: close");
client.println();
```

```
client.println("<!DOCTYPE html>");
client.println("<html>");
client.println("<head>");
client.println("<title>Arduino Web Page</title>");
client.println("</head>");
client.println("<body>");
client.println("<h1>Hello from Arduino!</h1>");
client.println("<p>A web page from the Arduino server</p>");
client.println("</body>");
client.println("</html>");
break;
}
if (c == '\n') {
currentLineIsBlank = true;
}
else if (c != '\r') {
currentLineIsBlank = false;
}
delay(1);
client.stop();
}
```

Then, upload the sketch to the Board.

Chapter Four:
Recent Information on Arduino Usage

Latest Arduino Information

Arduino has been used to create several unusual interactive objects across all walks of life and is still being improved to meet future human needs and challenges. Recently, the company said it developed four new Nano microcontroller Arduino boards for developers. The new boards—which come with several ready-to-use features—hit the market last July. The new boards are Nano 33 IOT, Nano BLE Sense, Nano 33 BLE, and Nano Every, and they are all compatible with the regular Nano boards.

The Nano Every is an ATMega4809 microcontroller designed to run at 20 MHz. It comes with a 4KB flash and 6KB RAM. The Nano 33 IOT is quite different from the Nano Every, as it runs at 48 MHz and is designed as a SAMD21G18A microcontroller. The board comes with Wi-Fi and Bluetooth connectivity, 32KB RAM, and a 256KB Flash. The board supports the Transport Layer Security (TLS) connections.

The Nano 33 BLE is suitable for short-range savvy projects because of its Bluetooth support system. With 256KB RAM and 1MB Flash, the board, which is designed as an nRF52480 microcontroller, can run at 64 MHz but only works with 3.3V input and output signals. The Nano 33 BLE Sense is suitable for gesture-based projects. Its sensors, which work for light, color, humidity, temperature, and gesture, make the Nano BLE Sense different from the Nano 33 BLE.

Pointers and How to Use them

Pointers are variables used to name or store a value for future use on the Arduino program. This value, which could be data retrieved from the sensor or other sources, is often used for mathematical calculations. All variables to be used for Arduino programming need to be declared first before one can commence executing projects. Declaring a variable is just identifying its type. Initializing the variable or assigning value to it may also be done when the variable is being reported. The size of the value to be stored will determine the type of variable to be used.

Variables should be declared where program functions can locate them quickly. This location is technically referred to as variable scope. The variable scope is a significant influence on how program functions are executed. Initializing a variable may not be compulsory when it is being declared, but the variable needs to be checked to see if it has valid data. Declared variables should only be used for intended purposes.

Variables are defined once they have been declared. Defining a variable is all about equalling the variable and value one wants to store via the assignment operator; the operator will instruct the system to carry out the instruction as desired. Codes are more readable when all variables carry descriptive names. Variables could be given any descriptive names but not the names in Arduino. A command like the one below can be used to declare a variable on the Arduino IDE.

Pointers—like other variables—have both identifiers and data types and play roles that are different from other variables. With an asterisk, we can tell the compiler to treat a variable as a pointer. A pointer indicates the data of another variable in the memory storage, not the variable itself. Data here refers to the set of information to be computed. A pointer can be considered a variable, but it does not store data; it only points to data already stored in the memory of the system. A defined pointer can be assigned the memory address of another variable if you want it to point to the variable. Pointers can be declared with "type* ptr; //" or "type *ptr; //" commands.

Programs do not necessarily have to be developed with pointers, but this will waste a lot of time during coding. Complex data types can be converted into bytes when one is using pointers, and this will speed up the coding exercise. A pointer is associated with two core values: memory address and data. While the memory address is saved in the pointer, the data is located within the memory address. Simply use the equals sign (=) when you want to modify the address. An asterisk can be used to access the data in the pointer's address. Dereferencing is the process of obtaining the data while the asterisk is the dereference operator.

The C "address-of" operator has vital information on how to use Arduino pointers. With an ampersand (&) symbol, known for standard variables, the operator would run functions that are strictly related to the pointer. With the ampersand, the program will receive a command to go for the address of the variable, not its value. So, you don't need to know the exact memory that houses the variable before you can place its address in the operator. Just use the pointer's operator and leave the compiler to handle the rest.

Both C and pointer variables hold varying values, but these values can be modified with arithmetic operations, such as addition, subtraction, increment, and decrement. One pointer can be subtracted from another if they have similar data types. While debugging your code, you may realize that the pointer arithmetic is not like regular arithmetic calculations. It's not exactly a straightforward concept, but it's nothing to worry about since the compiler can handle it.

Pointers and Arrays

Pointers and arrays share close connections. There is always a constant pointer to hold the starting address of a declared array. Also, the index notation for assessing elements in arrays works fine with pointers too. Pointers will be ideal for the two coding situations below.

1. **Pointers vs. Array:** We said earlier that pointers and arrays have a close connection. Pointers make dealing with data saved as arrays simple because they are an alternative channel for assessing such data. Routine coding is more convenient with pointers. Compilers come with highly sophisticated functions for extensive optimization, but they cannot push pointers aside because pointers make coding a pleasurable exercise while speeding up project execution.

2. **Passing Pointers to Functions:** Coding with C could look awkward at times unless functions are used extensively to write modular and organized codes. A function has one vital setback: it can't modify more than one variable, but pointers can. So, always use pointers to write code.

Pass pointers to functions by following these steps.

- Add a pointer as inputs in the function.

- Pass a variable's address to the function via the & operator.

The variable's address will equal the pointer's value, and the function will modify the variable's original value through the dereference operator. The code being run knows that the variable's value was changed.

C++ Pointers for Arduino

Programmers use functions, objects, arrays, and different variables to develop desired programs. Names will be given to all these variables during the declaration period, and they will be divided into bytes and saved in memory. The saved variables will have their addresses in the memory block where they are saved.

Pointers act as the beginning of the memory block where the bytes are housed. They can aid the passage of data via their reference roles and ensure that data processing is done, since it will not have to undergo the copying and pasting process. Pointers are used to allocate dynamic memory for arrays with unlimited size and aid the conversion of a data type to a byte stream. Each variable in C++ has its address in the &. There is an in-built function in the h header file of the Arduino that assigns dynamic memory to pointers. Indirect addressing of variables is possible when one obtains the value of the &, where the variable is saved. The indirect addressing operation uses * to read the value of the variable in the &.

Types of Pointers

Pointers to main types, pointers to arrays, pointers to functions, and pointers to void are the main types of pointers in use.

1. **Pointers to Main Types:** Pointers, like other variables, should be declared before being used. The * symbol comes before the name of the pointer to be declared. Find a way to make pointers appear differently to other variables. Allocation of required bytes of

memory for the data type is done when pointers are declared.

2. **Pointers to Arrays:** Pointers aid project execution when one works with arrays. The array name—a hidden pointer—is aimed at the first element of the array. Pointers to arrays can be used conveniently by programmers to write code and run other functions.

3. **Pointers to Functions:** Pointers to functions are convenient to use because the function name is just another pointer. The code is located in the memory address of its program. This memory address is stored by a pointer to function and gives the pointer control over the memory address. To run this process, use pointers to:

    - Access a variable and its address

    - Transfer the name of one function to another.

4. **Pointers to Void:** Pointers to void refers to objects with no defined types, which are pointed out by pointers when different data types are being stored in a single memory cell. However, explicit conversion of objects to the desired data type must be done before the pointer to void can be used.

The compiler executes the task of allocating required memory cells to a declared variable. The cells can only run intended functions, even when the declared variable has been discarded and thus earned itself the static name variable. One static variable may be removed to accommodate another one that needs a significant amount of memory. However, this is only possible when one is using dynamic variables. During program execution, dynamic variables can be created or deleted. No other variable except pointers can be used to access dynamic variables. The first element of the array can be removed with the operator delete [] command without any damage to other parts of the array.

Pointers' Operations

Simple operations such as indirect access, assignment, addition, subtraction, increment, decrement, comparison, and explicit type conversion can be performed with pointers.

The access operation is used to grant access to the variable's value of the address in the program index, whereas the * pointer name would provide the specific type of pointer to be declared. Pointers' arithmetic operations usually consider the size of the variable's type being used. The memory address will be increased by 1 byte when the pointer runs an increment operation on the chart data type. For a long data type, the increment operation would cause 4 bytes to be added to its memory address. Arithmetic operations are mainly used for arrays and other sequential data in the memory.

Conversion of Data Types to Bytes

A variable of data types should be converted to separate bytes to create a non-volatile memory to write in. This action will only take 2 bytes of memory, and you can use the pointer to do it.

Run the steps below to read a byte.

1. Get the address of the variable via the & operator
2. Convert the address to the * type byte
3. Apply indirect addressing operation
4. Add 1 to the pointer to read the second byte

Pointers play essential roles in Arduino programming, but you need to define them before you can use them to convert astronomical data to bytes, since this will aid speedy execution of the program.

Chapter Five: Arduino Coding Principles

Minimum Coding Requirement

Arduino IDE is used to write codes or sketches to build amazing hardware projects. These codes are compiled and uploaded to the Arduino boards for prompt execution. Arduino IDE and boards, which have been discussed in the previous chapters, are the minimum coding requirement for executing Arduino hardware projects. Coding involves the calling of the setup function to initialize libraries, pin modes, and other variables necessary for writing a sketch. The loop function takes over shortly when the setup has initialized other operations. All the loop function does is ensure that programs run and respond to change.

This change takes the form of commands, and the loop section within the sketch controls the board to run specific operations. Users need not worry about the code at the bottom of the sketch because it runs no particular function other than copying, pasting, and providing tips on how to write comments. Users should look out for lines that start with two slashes (//). Nothing should be written on such lines because the compiler cannot read anything there. Some functional codes carry the two slashes to shut comments, and you can use the slashes to program your codes to step-by-step. You and other people can now understand the step-by-step phase of the project.

Arduino Libraries: The Arduino library houses mainly C++ code files and C++ header files. The header files show the structure of the library, its variables, and its function, whereas the code files would implement the functions. Arduino has built-in libraries, where users can access basic program features and functionalities. Also, users can import program features and capabilities from other libraries to complement what is readily available on the Arduino built-in libraries.

Libraries are available for download online, but every user must decide on the one to use first. Since libraries flood the internet, one may be confused about which one to download. Open your Arduino IDE after you have the library downloaded. Click on Sketch >Include Library >Manage Libraries and choose the library to import to the Arduino IDE. Wait for the process to finish, and the library will appear in the sketch menu. In comparison, some of these libraries address new functions; others will centre on specific components of Arduino.

Pin Definitions: Arduino pins need to be defined before you can use them. The functionality (input or output) features of each pin will be made known, and you can do this with the "#define pinNamepinNumber" command.

Debugging Arduino Code

Coding is a creative exercise. You should do it cautiously to avoid debugging issues. Although it may not work as intended at first, there is room for adjustment. Debugging—an essential part of Arduino coding—appears difficult since Arduino does not have a customized debugging tool. At the same time, some programs come with a debugger to track bugs and correct them. The absence of a debugger on the Arduino IDE makes Arduino project management more challenging. Programmers cannot see how the codes run or locate track bugs when working on the Arduino IDE but have access to few progress messages via their device serial monitor or LED screen.

Arduino code debugging is quite different from computer code debugging. Arduino codes use physical inputs to control tangible outputs, and this justifies the look-out for alternative methods and tools to debug the codes. Everything, from code debugging on Arduino to aiding Arduino debugging via a simulator, is explained carefully through the building phases below. With this, you can write working codes.

Design: The project's design is as important as the project itself. Special care is required to select the right components for the project, or the whole idea is defeated. A clear mental picture of the project is all one needs to choose these components. For example, anyone who plans to run a code to light up LEDs should lay its foundation well in the project design phase. How the sketches and circuits work will ultimately affect the outlooks of the project.

Build: Circuits aid projects' building by helping the Arduino IDE send the C++ machine code to the board.

Circuit.io Code: One can get a test code here. Although this code has no logic, you can use it to check whether all components are wired correctly or function well. This code can aid hardware capacity to run desired projects. Also, access to chosen components' code libraries is available in the circuit.io platform. The debugging process can run once the test code fails. Follow the simple steps below to run the debugging process effortlessly.

1. **Check your hardware:** Arduino code debugging can only work when the device is in good shape. Run the circuit.io test code to know the overall condition of your appliance. Go ahead to troubleshoot the device if the code does not work. We'll go over a few troubleshooting tricks to resolve the problem.

2. **Check the wiring:** Every wire on the circuit must be well-connected before Arduino code debugging can start. Take your time to check the circuit to be sure that cables are not connected to the wrong ports or pins on the Arduino board.

3. **Check soldering:** You may need to solder certain parts of the hardware during setup. Ensure that the soldering is done correctly because poorly soldered portions of the board will always result in technical issues.

4. **Check Power Supply:** Check the power supply to see whether it is connected properly. You may even use a multidiameter to check the power supply.

5. **Code Debugging:** Start writing your code if the test code works fine with your hardware. A few rules for efficient coding are presented here. Do follow the rules, so you will not have issues debugging your code.

    1. Write sketch in small chunks
    2. Test each sketch
    3. Give specific names to functions and variables
    4. Use functions
    5. Use constants, not numbers
    6. Create comments on coding choices for reference purpose

Pay close attention to the readability of code and proper indentation. Alternate-t may be used to create an auto-indentation effect on the sketch.

Compilation: A compilation error may surface when compiling or uploading code to the Arduino board. Failures of typos and syntax mainly cause the error. Particular attention should be given to these errors to avoid compilation issues. Messages of compilation errors can be seen in the bottom part of the software. The error messages may not be helpful, since they do not give an accurate or full description of the problem at hand. Fix the issues raised before you rerun the compilation process. Feel free to search for possible solutions on Google if the problem persists.

Common syntax errors include omitting a semicolon (;) at the end of each line; a misplaced parenthesis {}; typos; undefined variables; and functions. Click Run once you have solved the problem.

Run Code: Code debugging will start if an already-compiled code fails to run on the Board.

Serial Monitor: Decide on the parameters to hook the debugging process on and get them monitored on screen. With this, you can get an overview of the variables, input sensors, programs flow, and output values.

Check Code Manually: Running a manual check on the sketch will show the errors to be addressed in it. Follow these steps to check your code manually.

1. Write your sketch from scratch.

2. Break it to small chunks to identify possible errors.

3. Search your design to locate your main logic.

4. Check whether your code statements address your main logic.

5. Add more comments to your code to aid the running of the project.

Using External Software Debugging Tools: An advanced debugging tool may be used to address the problem if you cannot fix it manually with code. Although other IDEs come with debugging tools, Arduino does not have any. You have nothing to worry about because several external devices could make the Arduino code run entirely. Here are two advanced debugging tools for debugging codes on Arduino.

1. **Visual Micro:** This Microsoft advanced cross-platform plugin can create code for Arduino. Its ability to do library editing and share code makes it an excellent debugging tool for Arduino. Shared code can aid the build process, but the system will reject any code that is not compatible with Arduino. Visual Micro also runs Serial, Bluetooth, and Wi-Fi debugging.

2. **Atmel Studio:** This free IDE can be used to develop, compile, and upload a project to any microcontroller. It has terrific code error resolving facilities to aid code debugging, and it runs the same system with the Arduino IDE. It is a ready-to-use debugging tool for Arduino programmers.

Using Arduino Emulators and Simulators: You can use Arduino emulators and simulators to monitor and debug codes. Hobbyists and experts can use Arduino simulators to program, run, and test their ideas until they turn out perfect. Hardware simulation is a challenging process, and its debugging tools benefit only makers and hobbyists.

Debugging: Simulators can aid Arduino code debugging by correcting syntax and functional errors. One can write a sketch and test it with simulators. Simulators support the creation of electronic circuits needed to test the functionality of the plan. Simulators come with a few advantages: they help users see their codes in action, correct functional errors, run new systems, and identify areas for possible improvements. You may only use a simulator to correct non-functional errors, like a syntax error.

Plotting and Logging: Simulators can aid the plotting and logging of generated data into the Arduino program. You can use external software like Excel to explore the data and refine the content when you log the code to the program.

Experimentation: Users are more creative when they use simulators and emulators because they can experiment with their ideas easily in a virtual environment. Working outside simulators will confine users to static, theoretical knowledge and few ideas.

Debugging of Arduino code need not be a difficult task.

Chapter Six: Arduino C Data

What is it?

Little was known about the C programming language until 1983, when the X3J11 committee was formed by the American National Standard Institute (ANSI) to determine the acceptability or otherwise of the programming language. The language was accepted by the committee when the latter completed its analysis in 1989, and the International Organization for Standardization (ISO) also cast their support for the programming language. After that, the C programming language became known as "ANSI C" or "ISO C." Arduino C does not come with all the features of the standard C programming language.

Arduino C Data Types

Arduino C is quite similar to standard C data types. The compiler needs to know the kind of data that will go with every defined variable, so it can dedicate the right byte of memory for the variable. Value and reference are the two primary forms of data. There is a range of values for every variable defined with the value data type. Here is a tabular list of Arduino C data types, according to Purdum (2012, p. 37).

Type	Byte Length	Range of Values
Boolean	1	Limited to logic true and false
char	1	Range: −128 to +127
unsigned char	1	Range: 0 to 255
byte	1	Range: 0 to 255
int	2	Range: −32,768 to 32,767
unsigned int	2	Range: 0 to 65,535
word	2	Range: 0 to 65,535
long	4	Range: −2,147,483,648 to 2,147,483,647
unsigned long	4	Range: 0 to 4,294,967,295
float	4	Range: − 3.4028235E+38 to 3.4028235E+38
double	4	Range: − 3.4028235E+38 to 3.4028235E+38
string	?	A null ('\0') terminated reference type data build from a character array
String	?	A reference data type object
array	?	A sequence of a value type that is referenced by a single variable name
void	0	A descriptor used with functions as a return type when the function does not return a value

The Boolean Data Type

True or false are the only two values of the Boolean data type that a Boolean variable can assume when you define it in the compiler. See a valid definition of a Boolean variable in the example below:

Boolean my Switch = false;

The code above shows that the switch is on. Use the Boolean data type when you are dealing with a true or false variable.

The char Data Type

The char data type and unsigned char data type can store any character in an 8-bit form. For char data type, a negative value would go with one sign bit, but unsigned data types do not have any sign bit.

The byte Data Type

The byte data type—an 8-bit value like the char data type—comes with no sign bit but can store any value within a range of 0 and 255. This data type is beneficial for people who are running out of memory to store their data. Such people only need to change int data to byte to save the day.

The int Data Type

Both int and unsigned int data types accept only positive or negative whole numbers, and they have 16-bit value in Arduino C, unlike the 32-bit value commanded by int in other programming languages. Always consider the difference in the value of int when writing your code. Unsigned data types may increase the limit of positive values, but they cannot be used to save negative values. People prefer using the int data type in their programs.

The word Data Type

The range of values and storage requirements of the word data type and unsigned int are equal, but most programmers would always use unsigned int in the place of the word data type.

The long Data Type

The long data type accepts only whole numbers but consumes more storage memory. Consider using int instead of long if data values when the program is within the int value range, as this will speed up data movement and performance.

The float and double Data Types

Floating of numbers (fractional values) is allowed in Arduino C. Symbolic constants of fractional values expressed as PI, TWO-PI, etc., can be viewed at the Arduino.h header file situated in Arduino-1.0.1\hardware\Arduino\cores\Arduino. PI in the file is defined as:

#define PI 3.1415926535897932384626433832795

Use the code below if you want the compiler to assign the value above for your pi.

float pi = PI

Remember that pi and PI are different entities because C is case-sensitive. Float uses 4 bytes of storage memory for a value range of about 38 digits.

Double data type doubles float's storage memory requirement in most programming languages and therefore has a broader range of values. However, there is no difference between double and float data types in Arduino C, as both have 4 bytes of storage memory.

The string Data Type

A string data type is just a group of characters with a shared name. It often takes the form of array characters. You will know what an array is when we discuss array data type but let us see how a string is defined.

char my String [15];

Use the code can to allocate memory space for a string of 14 characters. It is 14 because there is a null termination byte or character at the end of the string. The Arduino C knows when and how to add the termination byte in the program. A string variable may be defined or initialized in any of these ways:

char name [] = "Daniel";

char name [7] = "Daniel";

In the first example, the compiler would have to decide the number of storage bytes to create. The compiler will then create 7 bytes of storage because the name has six characters and 1 for the null character. In the second example, the compiler was asked to create 7 bytes of storage.

String Data Type

The String data type has a capital "S" and is different from the string data type discussed earlier. This data type is an offshoot of the previous string data type that only has an object, not an array character. You can code this data type to aid the conversion of characters from lowercase to uppercase.

For example, you can convert a sequence of characters of a stored string variable named my File to uppercase letters with the command below:

my File = myFile.ToUpperCase();

Use the code below to allocate memory for the string if it has 39 characters.

String my File = String (40);

And if you want to convert the characters to lowercase letters, the code below can be used.

My File = myFile.ToLowerCase();

The void Data Type

The void data type is different from other data types we've gone over. It runs as a function and does not return any setup or loop values. It also takes all information directly to the compiler for prompt action and execution.

The array Data Type

Almost all the data types above can go with arrays. The array data type—being a composite data value—may have zero or more elements of a particular data type. Here are a few statements of array definitions.

int my File [15];

long my File [7];

float temp [200];

The statements above defined the specific array data type.

Decision Making in C

Arduino can aid program execution based on the information it receives from the programmer. It can accept input and read and take the necessary decisions to execute the desired action. Decision-making in Arduino C is mainly based on relational operators and if statements.

Relational Operators

The program knows that not all data has the same functions. So, to make the right decision, it compares two or more data at a time to come up with a better choice. Consider the relational operators in Arduino C below:

Operator	Interpretation
>	Greater than
>=	Greater than or equal to
<	Less than
<=	Less than or equal to
==	Equal to
!=	Not equal to

Relational operators will always come with logic true (non-zero) or logic false (zero) results. See the example below:

If x = 5 and y = 4, then:

x>y // Logic true

x<y // logic false

x == y // logic false

x != y // logic true

The if Statement

The CPU processes code instructions in a top-down manner, unless you give it a contrary command. You can make the setup () function assume the starting point for every Arduino C program, but this arrangement can be altered with the if statement. Consider the if statement example below:

int b = 8;

if (b <10) {

}

Based on the example above, b will first be defined and initialized to 8 before any general statement can run.

Program Loops in C

Many people hate repetitive tasks because they get bored when executing them. But whether the job is monotonous or otherwise, computers can perform it efficiently. Two things determine the functioning of a computer system: its overall condition and the correctness of instructions fed into it. With the right situation and direction, the computer will loop programs forever!

All program loops have a terminal point except the loop () function, which can run forever. The loop () in a running program can only be stopped by ending the current plan, uploading another program, pressing the reset button, or disconnecting the Arduino board from the power source. A program loop is well-behaved when you can use code to control it. A program loop must adhere to these conditions:

1. **Variable Initialization:** A loop simply means orderly execution of program statements, one after the other.

Variables have to be initialized to a familiar program state before you can execute the loop statements. Nothing determines statement loop iterations more than the value of variables awaiting initialization, but the control variable should stay as 0, or the loop variable will lose its natural state.

2. **Loop Control Test:** A great program loop will require no loop statements' iteration, but you have to run the loop control test to arrive at a well-behaved loop. Just make a loop variable to pass through a relational operator.

3. **Adjusting Loop Control Variable's State:** The control variable's state needs to change when loop statements are processed or the loop will run forever. Only the loop() function may run forever, not the code you create there.

Functions in C

A function is a set of codes that could solve a problem or execute a task. Functions—depending on areas of interest—are readily available in function libraries. These libraries are available for download on www.arduino.cc, the official website of Arduino, and they make Arduino programming very easy. These libraries come with time-tested codes for building great interactive projects. Save the stress and time involved in writing, testing, and debugging systems from scratch by using these rich function libraries.

Function Type Specifier

The function type specifier pops up once a function has been called or defined. It ensures that the returned data type is known. Depending on what the programmer wants, the returned data type could be long, char, double, int, or byte. However, should no value be returned, the specifier would have to opt for the void keyword.

Function Name

The identity of a function is its name. The name has to be short, simple, and straightforward. It must say what the task is all about. Use variables' naming rules to craft a functional signature for your Arduino C function.

Function Arguments

Next to the function name is an opening parenthesis, also known as function arguments or argument lists. The function would be bereft of required data for program execution if the function arguments were not well-stated. Function arguments can only send the data type they get from the function type specifier; however, if the programmer wrote an empty function, the void would be specified for the function. See the example below:

intbuyshoe;

intshoeperfoot;

intnumberofeet;

buyshoe= shoeneeded(shoeperfoot,numberoffeet);

In the example above, shoeperfoot and numberoffeet are the two function arguments for the shoeneeded() function.

Function Body

Next to function arguments is the function body. It would start with an opening brace "{" and ends with a closing brace "}" within the defined function. Every statement within this range remains the function body. The function body must have a return keyword if the function type specifier has a data value. See the example below:

intVolumeOfCylinder (int length, int width, int height)

{

int volume;

volume = length * width * height;

return volume;

}

In the example below, the function had a return statement in int because int was the function type specifier.

However, no return will be required when the function type specifier is void. See this example:

intVolumeOfCylinder (int length, int width, int height)

{

return length * width * height;

}

In the example above, the return value (the variable volume) was removed because the function type specifier was void.

Writing Your Functions

Visit http://arduino.cc/it/Reference/Libraries to check whether another person has already written the function you intend to write. Companies that sell Arduino shields and other hardware components often host source codes on their websites. Utilize these options to get the right code for your hardware projects. Write a function only when none are available to use.

Chapter Seven:
10 Great Beginners' Projects with Arduino

The Arduino board was a product of necessity. The urgent need to develop a fast prototyping tool for students of the Interactive Design Institute in Ivrea, Italy, gave birth to the development of Arduino in 2005. The 2005 experience is quite different from what is now available for use because the features and functions of the board have seen significant improvements. Arduino has been used extensively to build several unusual and physical interactive objects for human comfort, and more are still on the way. It makes no difference whether the user is a beginner or expert in programming. Anyone can use Arduino since it comes with easy-to-use features, and there are several online aids for beginners on the platform. Here are ten great Arduino projects for beginners.

1. Obstacle Avoiding Robot

Robots play surprising roles in our world. We even trust them with our lives because they hardly make mistakes like humans. This obstacle-avoiding robot—a product of Arduino and an ultrasonic sensor—is so intelligent that it does everything possible to prevent collisions and obstacles, even in unknown environments.

Components Required

- Arduino Nano

- HC-SR04 Ultrasonic Sensor

- LM298N Motor Driver Module
- 5V DC Motors
- Battery
- Wheels
- Chassis
- Jumper wires

Procedure

Define HC-SR04 trig and echo pins. Connect the trig pin to GPIO9 and echo pin to GPIO10 of the Arduino Nano and write this sketch:

int trigPin = 9;

int echoPin = 10;

Define LM298N Motor Driver Module pins for inputs. 4 data input pins are on the LM298N, and they control the direction of the connected motor. Add the code below to the sketch to define the module pins.

int revleft4 = 4;

int fwdleft5 = 5;

int revright6 = 6;

int fwdright7 = 7;

Define the direction of data in GPIO pins in setup (). Use the command below to set motor and tig pin as an output and Echo pin as an input.

pinMode (revleft4, OUTPUT);

pinMode (fwdleft5, OUTPUT);

pinMode (revright6, OUTPUT);

pinMode (fwdright7, OUTPUT);

pinMode (trigpin, OUTPUT);

pinMode (echoPin, INPUT);

Get the HC-SR04 distance of motor direction in loop() function. The distance at which the device can sense an obstacle is the motor direction. Add the code below to the sketch to perfect this stage.

digitalWrite (trigPin, LOW);

delayMicroseconds (2);

digitalWrite (trigPin, HIGH);

delayMicroseconds (10);

duration = pulseIn (echoPin, HIGH);

distance = duration / 58.2;

delay (10);

Instruct the device to move forward when there is an obstacle by adding this command to the sketch.

if (distance > 19)

{

digitalWrite (fwdright7, HIGH);

digitalWrite (revright6, LOW);

digitalWrite (fwdleft5, HIGH);

digitalWrite (revleft4, LOW);

}

Instruct the device to stop and avoid obstacles by adding this command to the sketch.

if (distance < 18)

{

digitalWrite (fwdright7, LOW);

digitalWrite (revright6, LOW);

digitalWrite (fwdleft5, LOW);

digitalWrite (revleft4, LOW);

delay (500);

digitalWrite (fwdright7, LOW);

digitalWrite (revright6, HIGH);

digitalWrite (fwdleft5, LOW);

digitalWrite (revleft4, HIGH);

delay (500);

digitalWrite (fwdright7, LOW);

digitalWrite (revright6, LOW);

digitalWrite (fwdleft5, LOW);

digitalWrite (revleft4, LOW);

delay (100);

digitalWrite (fwdright7, HIGH);

digitalWrite (revright6, LOW);

digitalWrite (revleft4, LOW);

digitalWrite (fwdleft5, LOW);

delay (500);

}

Upload sketch to the Board

2. Text-to-Speech Converter

Arduino text-to-speech converter aids the conversion of text to spoken speech via an electronic device. Large organizations and public transportation companies use the tool often to interact or pass information to their customers.

Components Required

- Arduino Uno
- Connecting Wires
- 10K Resistor
- An Amplifier Circuit
- A Speaker

Procedure

Connect 10K resistor to digital three pins of your Arduino. Plug power supply to the amplifier circuit and connect the Arduino board to the circuit before you connect the speaker. Add Arduino TTS library on the IDE. To do this, open Sketch

>Include Library >Manage Libraries and add the TTS library. Type Talkie in the Search bar to install the library.

Include some headers and convert digital pin 3 to output pin by writing this command in Sketch.

#include "Talkie.h"

#include "Vocab_US_Large.h"

#include "Vocab_Special.h"

Make setup () empty and activate loop () with these commands

void setup () {

}

void loop () {

voice.say (spPAUSE2);

voice.say (sp2_DANGER);

voice.say (sp2_DANGER);

voice.say (sp3_STORM);

voice.say (sp3_IN);

voice.say (sp3_THE);

voice.say (sp3_NORTH);

}

Upload Sketch to the Arduino board

3. Weather Station

This simple weather station can be powered with the DHT11 sensor and Arduino to sense humidity and temperature and provide results via its LCD Display. DHT11—the humidity and temperature sensor—may have three or four pins, depending on the type one purchases in the market. You can use the two DHT11 sensor types for this project.

Components Required

- DHT11
- 16×2 12C LCD Display
- Arduino Uno
- 8 Male or Female Jumper Wires
- Connect DHT11 to the Arduino board

Procedure

Use the connection sample below if you are using a DHT11 sensor with four pins.

DHT11	Arduino Uno
VCC	3.3V
OUT	Pin4 (Digital)
GND	GND
NC	--

Ensure you connect a 10K Ohm resistor between the DHT11 VCC and the Out Pin.

Use the sample below to connect DHT11 with three pins.

DHT11	Arduino Uno
VCC	3.3V
OUT	Pin 4 (Digital)
GND	GND

Connect the LCD Display to Arduino

The LCD consists of SCL and SDA signals. Although SCL represents the clock signal, the SDA shows the data signals. There is a current bus master in the LCD that generates the clock signal, but specific forces may prevent the bus master from creating the required data. Consider the sample below when connecting the LCD Display.

LCD Display	Arduino
GND	GND
VCC	5V
SDA	A4
SCL	A5

Create the Code

Ensure the DHT11 and 12C LCD libraries are downloaded and included. The DHT11 library is available for download on https://mega.nz/file/4XZ2CaAT#AhhLE0CUN7XMrgzAuAtFF UA9BucotUSD3-to4qEJr2c, and you can download the 12C LCD from https://drive.google.com/file/d/1edC9yXdDUFs59nwzDIsCZ W2gma3xkgBQ/view. Write the command below in the Sketch once you have included the libraries.

#include <dht.h>

```
#include <Wire.h>

#include <Liquid Crystal_12C.h>

LiquidCrystal_12C lcd(0×27, 2, 1, 0, 4, 5, 6, 7, 3, POSITIVE);

dht DHT; #define DHT11_PIN 4

void setup(){

lcd.begin(16, 2); }

void loop () {

int d = DHT.read 11 (DHT11_PIN);

lcd.setCursor(0,0);

lcd.print("Temp: ");

lcd.print(DHT.temperature);

lcd.print((char)223);

lcd.print("C");

lcd.setCursor(0, 1);

lcd.print("Humidity: ");

lcd.print(DHT.humidity);

lcd.print("%");

delay(1000);

}
```

Upload Sketch to the Arduino board.

4. Cough Detection System

Cough and noise sounds are look-alikes, but you can use the cough detection system to differentiate cough from noise. The Arduino 33 BLE Sense powers the system. With the aid of the Edge Impulse Studio, the Arduino device can show whether a sound is caused by noise or cough.

Components Required

- Arduino 33 BLE Sense
- LED
- Jumper Wires

Procedure

Connect LED Positive lead to Arduino 33 BLE Sense digital pin four and Negative point to Arduino GND pin. Collect samples of cough and noise for the Arduino and create "cough" and "noise" classes of the dataset. Create an account on the Edge Impulse website to create the courses of the dataset. Use your cell phone to load the samples from the Edge Impulse Studio. To connect your cell phone, Click on Devices >Connect a New Device >Use your Mobile Phone. Scan the QR code that appears with your cell phone and get your cell phone connected to the Studio.

Click on Data acquisition page >enter label name >choose microphone as sensor >enter sample length to load the samples. To start sampling coughs, feel free to use online cough samples. Click on the Start sampling button to record 10 to 12 cough samples of different lengths.

Repeat the process to get 10 or 12 noise samples and create an impulse for the data by clicking on Create impulse page. Click on Add a processing block >Audio (MFCC) block >Add a learning block >Neural Network (Keras) block >Save Impulse. Visit the MFCC page. Click on Generate Features to create MFCC blocks for all audio samples. Click NN Classifier page >three dots (...) over the Neural Network settings >and Switch to Keras mode.

Click on Deployment page >Arduino Library >Build to create the Arduino library for the project. Add the library to your IDE. Open Sketch >Include Library >Add.ZIP library and load your saved samples by clicking on File >Examples >Project name – Edge Impulse >nano_ble33_sense_microphone.

Open Sketch and program the commands below.

```
#define EIDSP_QUANTIZE_FILTERBANK 0
#include <PDM.h>
#include <ashish3121-project-1_inference.h>
#define led 5
typedefstruct{
int16_t *buffer;
uint8_t buf_ready;
uint32_t buf_count;
uint32_t n_samples;
} inference_t;
staticinference_t inference;
staticboolrecord_ready = false;
staticsignedshortsampleBuffer[2048];
```

```
static bool debug_nn = false;

void setup()
{
    Serial.begin(115200);
    pinMode(led, OUTPUT);
    ei_printf("Inferencing settings:\n");
    ei_printf("\tInterval: %.2f ms.\n", (float)EI_CLASSIFIER_INTERVAL_MS);
    ei_printf("\tFrame size: %d\n", EI_CLASSIFIER_DSP_INPUT_FRAME_SIZE);
    ei_printf("\tSample length: %d ms.\n", EI_CLASSIFIER_RAW_SAMPLE_COUNT / 16);
    if(microphone_inference_start(EI_CLASSIFIER_RAW_SAMPLE_COUNT) == false) {
        ei_printf("ERR: Failed to setup audio sampling\r\n");
        return;
    }
}

void loop()
{
    ei_printf("Starting inferencing in 2 seconds...\n");
    delay(2000);
    ei_printf("Recording...\n");
    bool m = microphone_inference_record();
```

```
    if(!m) {

    ei_printf("ERR: Failed to record audio...\n");

    return;

    }

    ei_printf("Recording done\n");

    signal_t signal;

    signal.total_length = EI_CLASSIFIER_RAW_SAMPLE_COUNT;

    signal.get_data = &microphone_audio_signal_get_data;

    ei_impulse_result_t result = { 0 };

    EI_IMPULSE_ERROR r = run_classifier(&signal, &result, debug_nn);

    if(r != EI_IMPULSE_OK) {

    ei_printf("ERR: Failed to run classifier (%d)\n", r);

    return;

    }

    ei_printf("Predictions (DSP: %d ms., Classification: %d ms., Anomaly: %d ms.): \n",

    result.timing.dsp, result.timing.classification, result.timing.anomaly);

    for(size_t ix = 1; ix < EI_CLASSIFIER_LABEL_COUNT; ix++) {

    Serial.print( result.classification[ix].value);

    floatData = result.classification[ix].value;

    if(Data < 0.50){
```

```
        Serial.print("Cough Detected");
        alarm();
      }
    }
    // ei_printf("    %s: %.5f\n", result.classification[ix].label, result.classification[ix].value);
    // }
    #if EI_CLASSIFIER_HAS_ANOMALY == 1
    ei_printf(" anomaly score: %.3f\n", result.anomaly);
    #endif
}

void ei_printf(const char *format, ...) {
    static char print_buf[1024] = { 0 };
    va_list args;
    va_start(args, format);
    int r = vsnprintf(print_buf, sizeof(print_buf), format, args);
    va_end(args);
    if(r > 0) {
        Serial.write(print_buf);
    }
}

static void pdm_data_ready_inference_callback(void)
{
```

```
intbytesAvailable = PDM.available();

intbytesRead = PDM.read((char*)&sampleBuffer[0], bytesAvailable);

if(record_ready == true|| inference.buf_ready == 1) {

inference.buffer[inference.buf_count++] = sampleBuffer[i];

if(inference.buf_count >= inference.n_samples) {

inference.buf_count = 0;

inference.buf_ready = 1;

}

staticboolmicrophone_inference_start(uint32_t n_samples)

{

inference.buffer = (int16_t *)malloc(n_samples * sizeof(int16_t));

if(inference.buffer == NULL) {

returnfalse;

}

inference.buf_count = 0;

inference.n_samples = n_samples;

inference.buf_ready = 0;

PDM.onReceive(&pdm_data_ready_inference_callback);

PDM.setGain(80);

PDM.setBufferSize(4096);
```

```
// - a 16 kHz sample rate
if(!PDM.begin(1, EI_CLASSIFIER_FREQUENCY)) {
ei_printf("Failed to start PDM!");
}
record_ready = true;
returntrue;
}
staticboolmicrophone_inference_record(void)
{
inference.buf_ready = 0;
inference.buf_count = 0;
while(inference.buf_ready == 0) {
delay(10);
}
returntrue;
}
staticintmicrophone_audio_signal_get_data(size_toffset, size_tlength, float*out_ptr)
{
arm_q15_to_float(&inference.buffer[offset], out_ptr, length);
return0;
}
staticvoidmicrophone_inference_end(void)
```

```
{
PDM.end();
free(inference.buffer);
}
#error "Invalid model for current sensor."
#endif
voidalarm(){
for(size_tt = 0; t < 4; t++) {
digitalWrite(led, HIGH);
delay(1000);
digitalWrite(led, LOW);
delay(1000);
//  digitalWrite(led, HIGH);
//  delay(1000);
//  digitalWrite(led, LOW);
}
```

Upload the code to the board.

5. Rain Detector System

The rain detector system is an interface between an Arduino and rain sensor. Use the device to harness rainfall data to assist farmers in planning an effective irrigation system.

Components Required

- Arduino Uno

- Rain Sensor
- Buzzer
- Connecting Wires
- Procedure

Procedure

Connect buzzer to Digital pin five and rain sensor to Analog pin 0 before you plug the Arduino board to a power supply system.

Define pin five as a buzzer and pin A0 as rainfall by writing these commands in the Sketch.

#define rainfall A0

#define buzzer 5

int value;

int set = 10;

Set buzzer output pin, rainfall input pin, and initialize serial communication by adding these commands.

void setup() {

Serial.begin(9600);

pinMode(buzzer, OUTPUT);

pinMode(rainfall, INPUT);

}

Instruct analogRead to read the value of the rain sensor from 0 to 225. Add these commands to achieve that.

```
void loop() {

value = analogRead(rainfall);

Serial.printing(value);

value = map(value,0,1023,225,0);
```

Instruct the program to loop when the sensor value is higher than the set amount. Do this by adding the command below.

```
if(value> =set){

Serial.printing("rain detected");

digitalWrite(buzzer,HIGH);
```

Instruct the program to enter an else function when an obtained value is not up to the set value. Add the command below.

```
else{

digitalWrite(buzzer, LOW);
```

Upload the code to the Arduino board.

6. Coin Sorting Machine

Arduino sorting machine works with IR sensors to deliver rare coins counting and sorting experience for users. Its output—the total value of counted coins—will be displayed via a 16×2 LCD Display.

Components Required

- Arduino Uno
- IR Sensor

- Breadboard
- 16×2 Alphanumeric LCD
- 12C Module for 16x2 Alphanumeric LCD
- Connecting Wires

Procedure

Mark each coin size in cardboard and cut out the marked portion accurately. Insert each coin in the hole on the cardboard. Calibrate IR sensors close to the output path of each coin. Use the 12C module to connect the LCD to the Arduino. Add the LiquidCrystal_12C.h library. To add this library, go to Sketch >Include library >Manage libraries.

Enter the command below in your sketch.

#include <Wire.h>

#include <LiquidCrystal_12C.h>

LiquidCrystal_12C lcd(0×27,16,2);

Instruct LCD to show welcome message via setup() by adding the command below.

lcd.init();

lcd.backlight();

lcd.setCursor(0,0);

lcd.print(" ARDUINO BASED.   ");

lcd.setCursor(0,1);

lcd.print(" COIN SORTING ");

delay(2000);

lcd.clear();

Add this command to store sensor values in different variables.

int s1=analogRead(A0);

int s2=analogRead (A1);

int s3=analogRead(A2);

Increment the counter values of coins with this command.

If(s1>=200 &&f1==0)

{

f1=0

}

else if(s1 <200 && f1==1)

{

f1=0;

c1++;

}

Add these commands to display count values through LCD.

lcd.set(Cursor(0,0);

lcd.print("RS10 RS2 RS5");

lcd.setCursor(1,1);

lcd.print(c1);

lcd.setCursor(7,1);

lcd.print(c2);

lcd.setCursor(14,1);

lcd.print(c3);

Upload sketch to Arduino board

7. Arduino Door Lock System

The Arduino door lock system is built with Radio Frequency Identification (RFID) to control access to homes and offices.

Components Required

- Arduino Uno
- RFID-RC522 Module
- 12V Solenoid Lock
- Hall Effect Sensor
- Relay Module
- 10K Resistor
- Buzzer

Procedure

Plug the positive pin of the buzzer in Arduino digital pin 4, connect GND pin to Arduino ground pin, use 10K resistor between VCC and OUT pins, and plug the solenoid lock to Arduino via the relay module.

Use this information to run the connection.

RFID Pin	Arduino Uno Pin
SDA	Digital 10
SCK	Digital 13
MOSI	Digital 11
MISO	Digital 12
IRQ	Unconnected
GND	GND
RST	Digital 9
3.3V	3.3V
Hall Effect Sensor Pin	Arduino Uno Pin
5V	5V

Add these commands to define the RFID module, Solenoid lock, and Buzzer pins.

int Buzzer = 4;

constintLockPin= 2;

#define SS_PIN 10

#define RST_PIN 9

Add the commands below to make Lock pin and Buzzer output, Hall Effect sensor as input, and launch SPI communication.

pinMode(LockPin, OUTPUT);

pinMode(Buzzer, OUTPUT);

pinMode(hall_sensor, INPUT);

SPI.begin();

mfrc522.PCD_Init();

Add the command to read values of the hall sensor in the void loop.

state = digitalRead(hall_sensor);

Serial.print(state);

Delay(3000);

If(state==LOW){

digitalWrite(LockPin, LOW);

Serial.print("Door Closed");

digitalWrite(Buzzer, HIGH);

delay(2000);

digitalWrite(Buzzer, LOW);}

Add the command below in a void loop to know if a new RFID card is available.

if (! mfrc522.PICC_IsNewCardPresent())

{

return;

}

// Select UID on of the cards

```
if ( ! mfrc522.PICC_ReadCardSerial())

{

return;

}

String content= "";

byte letter;

for (byte i = 0; i< mfrc522.uid.size;i++)

{

content.concat(String(mfrc522.uid.uidByte[i] < 0×10 ? " 0" :" "));

content.concat(String(mfrc522.uid.uidByte[i], HEX));

}
```

Add these commands to complete the process

```
Serial.printing();

Serial.print("Message : ");

content.toUpperCase();

if (content.substring(1) == "60 4E 07 1E" );

{

digitalWrite(LockPin, HIGH);

Serial.print("Door Unlocked ");

digitalWrite(Buzzer, HIGH);
```

```
delay(2000);

digitalWrite(Buzzer, LOW);

}

else

{

Serial.printIn("You are not Authorized");

digitalWrite(Buzzer, HIGH);

delay(2000);

digitalWrite(Buzzer, LOW);

}

{
```

Upload sketch to the board

8. Arduino Solar Tracker

Arduino solar tracker is a beautiful device that you can use to gather data on rays of sunlight in a place over some time.

Components Required

- Arduino Uno
- Servo Motor
- Light Sensors
- Four LDRs
- Perforated Metal Strip
- Four 100KΩ Resistors

Procedure

Use a voltage divider to connect LDRs and the resistors and send output to Arduino 4 analog pins, with Arduino digital pins 9 and 10 acting as the PWM inputs. Design a hole in the middle of the cardboard and four holes in its sizes. Fit the LDRs to the holes. Attach the solar panel and bring out its two wires through the middle hole.

Trim one out of the 2 LDRs leads to make it shorter. Bend the metal strip to fit into the back of the cardboard. Use glue to fix the LDRs firmly. Solder LDRs two heads with other ends of LDRs resistor and use a wire to connect the four heads of the LDRs.

Connect outputs of the LDRs to the Arduino board with bus wire and insert the cable into the metal strip. Solder the wires to the meeting point of the LDRs and resistor. Supply VCC and GND to the LDR circuit by inserting two new wire buses in the metal strip. Solder one wire to LDRs leads (those connected with resistors) and the other wire to other points. Use Screw to join a service motor to the metal strip and apply glue to fix it firmly.

Open your Sketch and run this command to include Servo motor.

```
#include <Servo.h>

Servo servohori;

intservoh = 0;

intservohLimitHigh = 160;

intservohLimitLow = 20;

Servo servoverti;

intservov = 0;

intservovLimitHigh= 160;

intservovLimitLow = 20;
```

Assign LDRs with this command

```
intIdrtopl= 2;

intIdrtopl = 1;

intIdrbotl= 3;

intIdrbotr = 0;

void setup()

{

servohori.attach(10);
```

servohori.write(0);

servoverti.attach(9);

servoverti.write(0);

delay(500);

}

void loop()

{

servoh= servohori.read();

servov = servoverti.read();

Add this command to capture analog values of the LDRs.

inttopl = analogRead(Idrtopl);

inttopr = analogRead(Idrtopl);

intbotl = analogRead(Idrbotl);

inbotr = analogRead(Idrbotr);

Add this command to calculate the average.

intavgtop = (topl + topr);

intavgbot = (botl + botr);

intavgleft = (topl + botl);

intavgright = (topr + botr);

if (avgtop<avgbot)

{

```
servoverti.write(servov +1);
if (servov>servovLimitHigh)
{
servov = servovLimitHigh;
}
delay(10);
{
else if (avgbot<avgtop)
}
servoverti.write(servov -1);
if (servov<servovLimitLow)
servov = servovLimitLow;
}
delay(10);
}
else
{
servoverti.write(servov);
}
if (avgleft>avgright)
{
```

```
servohori.write(servoh +1);

}

if (servoh>servohLimitHigh)

{

servoh = servohLimitHigh;

}

delay(10);

else if (avgright>avgleft)

servohori.write(servoh -1);

if (servoh<servohLimitLow)

{

servoh = servohLimitLow;

}

delay(10);

}

else

{

servohori.write(servoh);

}
```

Upload the sketch to the board.

9. Home Alarm System

The Arduino home alarm system is one cool project every beginner can do to secure home, prevent theft and theft attempts, and alert people when intruders gain access to their homes and properties.

Components Required

- Ultrasonic Sensor
- Arduino Uno
- Piezo Buzzer
- Breadboard
- LED
- Jumper Wires

Procedure

Connect the Ultrasonic sensor. GDN pin goes to the Breadboard Ground railings, VCC pin to Positive fences of the Breadboard, Echo pin to Arduino Digital pin 9, while the Trig in will go to Arduino Digital pin 10. Connect the Piezo Buzzer. Connect the red wire to Digital pin 13 and the ground wire to the Breadboard negative railings.

Connect the LED. Anode and cathode are the two terminals of LED. The anode is longer than the cathode. Connect Anode to Digital pin 13, while cathode should go to the Breadboard negative railings.

Write the command below in the Sketch to complete the interface.

constinttrigPin= 9;

```
constintechoPin= 10;

constint buzzer = 11;

constintledPin = 13;

long duration;

int distance;

int safetyDistance;

void setup() {

pinMode(trigPin, OUTPUT);

pinMode(echoPin, INPUT);

pinMode(buzzer, OUTPUT);
```

Add the commands below to create the alarm system.

```
pinMode(ledPin, OUTPUT);

Serial.begin(9600);

}

Void loop() {

digitalWrite(trigPin, LOW);

delayMicroseconds(2);

digitalWrite(trigPin, HIGH);

delayMicroseconds(10);

digitalWrite(trigPin, LOW);

duration = pulseIn(echoPin, HIGH);
```

```
distance = duration*0.034/2;

safetyDistance = distance;

if (safetyDistance<= 5){

digitalWrite(buzzer, HIGH);

digitalWrite(ledPin, HIGH);

}

else{

digitalWrite(buzzer, LOW);

digitalWrite(ledPin, LOW);}

Serial.print("Distance: ");

Serial.println(distance);

}
```

Upload the sketch to the Arduino board

10. Arduino 3-Way Traffic Light

Arduino 3-way traffic light is a sensation! It is a beauty to behold, although its role is to aid orderly control of humans and vehicular movements on roads. One great thing about this light is that it is effortless to build.

Components Required

- LED Lights (three red, three green, and three yellow)
- Three 220ohm Resistors
- Breadboard
- Male to Female Connectors
- Arduino Uno

Procedure

Plug LEDs in the breadboard in Red, Green, and Yellow order. Connect LEDs negative terminals to the resistor, one after the other, as well as the connector wires. Plug each cable consecutively to Arduino from Digital pins 2 – 10 and use Arduino 5V and GND pins to power the breadboard.

Add the command below to the Sketch to configure output pins.

void setup() {

pinMode(2,OUTPUT);

pinMode(3,OUTPUT);

pinMode(4,OUTPUT);

pinMode(5,OUTPUT);

pinMode(6,OUTPUT);

pinMode(7,OUTPUT);

pinMode(8,OUTPUT);

pinMode (9,OUTPUT);

pinMode (10,OUTPUT);

}

Add the command below in void loop() to turn light on and off in sequence.

void loop()

{

digitalWrite(2,1);

digitalWrite(7,1);

digitalWrite(10,1);

digitalWrite(4,0);

digitalWrite(3,0);

digitalWrite(6,0);

digitalWrite(8,0);

digitalWrite(9,0);

digitalWrite(5,0);

delay(5000);

To enable the yellow lights, add this command.

digitalWrite(3,1);

digitalWrite(6,1);

digitalWrite(2,0);

digitalWrite(7,0);

delay(1000);

Add the command below to enable second signals.

digitalWrite(4,1);

digitalWrite(10,1);

digitalWrite(2,0);

digitalWrite(6,0);

digitalWrite(8,0);

digitalWrite(9,0);

digitalWrite(7,0);

delay(5000)

Enable yellow lights by adding this command.

digitalWrite(9,1);

digitalWrite(6,1);

digitalWrite(10,0);

digitalWrite(4,0);

delay(1000);

Upload the Sketch to the Arduino board.

Chapter Eight: Fixing Common Arduino Troubleshooting Problems

Common Arduino Issues

A few troubleshooting challenges have been recorded by people who use microcontrollers to build physical interactive objects in the recent past, and users of Arduino are not immune to these challenges. However, beginners with no prior electronics background will have more ways to address these challenges as they pop up. This is not a reason to be scared or worried or abandon the beautiful objects one intends to build. Some of these challenges are not as complicated as they appear. There are simple steps that users can take to fix some of these troubleshooting issues without finding help elsewhere. Here, we will consider common Arduino troubleshooting problems and what to do to get them fixed.

Arduino Board is not Recognized

Connection is crucial for people who are using Arduino to run their projects. Do the wiring carefully and make sure that everything is in the right place because connection issues can prevent the computer from recognizing the Arduino board. When the computer fails to recognize the board, the user will have problems uploading their codes. The issue occurred because the user was unable to list their Arduino board in one of the Arduino IDE's ports lists. Users of cheap Arduino clones with CH340g USB or Serial converter chip experience this problem more than those who purchased their boards from

Arduino. So, make sure you buy the original Arduino board from www.arduino.cc, the official website of Arduino.

Users of Standard Arduino boards may experience this hitch since the boards come with USB and Serial drivers too. You can install these drivers when you install the Arduino IDE; however, this troubleshooting issue will be fixed when you recognize the cause of the problem. All the user needs to do is get the driver for the chip downloaded and installed via the Arduino website if they want to use the USB or Serial converter to connect their Arduino boards. Locating the port to list or connecting the board on the IDE becomes easy once the driver has been downloaded and installed. Follow these steps to download and install the missing drivers.

1. Download drivers for USB and Serial Chips from www.arduino.cc.
2. Click on Install>Allow Installation if the operating system prompts a warning signal.
3. Wait for Installation to complete and click Finish.
4. Restart the computer and launch your Arduino software.

Unable to Upload Code

Users cannot achieve their program goals if they cannot upload their codes. This problem can be frustrating for people whose search for a fantastic microcontroller for physical interactive objects led them to Arduino. The frustration could be so devastating that such people would consider quitting the project. This issue will occur when the setting of your Arduino IDE is not compatible with your board. Upload issues will persist until you select the correct port and board in the Tools menu of your Arduino IDE. Just check the Boards Manager to look for your Arduino board if it is not available on the list of boards in your IDE.

Board Not in Sync

This issue hinders code uploading and threatens the effort already injected into the work. At times, users will be greeted with the "Done uploading" display, only to see the IDE prompt the "avrdude: stk500_getsync(): not in sync: resp=*0x00*" error code. This code shows that the Atmega chip on the Arduino board is not working, and some issues may have caused the problem. Clear the problem by running the few steps below.

1. Check digital pins 0 and 1 and make sure nothing is connected there.
2. Check the Tools menu to see whether you have selected the right port.
3. Reset the Arduino board and try to upload the code again.
4. Disconnect and reconnect the board to the computer.
5. Restart the Arduino IDE.

Use another board on the computer or test your board on another computer if the above steps failed to yield the desired result. You can reinstall the Arduino IDE or use Arduino firmware to flash the board. This firmware is available for download on the official website of Arduino. Consider buying another Arduino board if the problem persists.

Code Fails to Start on Power Reset

This issue occurs when the Arduino board reverts to sketch rather than running the uploaded sketch when you press the reset button. Like some other troubleshooting issues, many factors could be responsible for this hitch. You may check your code to see whether it is correct or review the serial data to see if it is not programmed to send a sketch the very moment it comes on. The board will hang if the serial data submits a plan once it comes online, the board will hang or stay idle. Find a way to delay the operation of the serial data to address this issue. Delaying the serial data may not be suitable for some projects. An external programmer can be used to upload the codes of such projects directly to the board, being a way to bypass the bootloader.

Unable to Set Host COM Port Automatically

This error will pop up when you disconnect your Arduino board from the computer or when it is not recognized. Check the connection to see whether you have done it correctly. If not, get the board connected and wait for the operating system to run the installation process. Try resolving the Arduino board driver if the error popped up when the board was switched on and correctly connected to the computer. This issue is common to Windows, but you can resolve it with these steps.

1. Click Start menu >Select Devices and Printers >Other Devices or COM ports >Unknown Device.

2. Double click Unknown Device >Click Hardware >Properties >Update Driver Software.

3. Click Browse my Computer for Driver Software >Choose Include subfolders.

4. Click Browse >Select Installation Folder (the one that supports your Arduino board) >Click Next.

5. Click Install this driver anyway, and wait for Windows to finish installing the driver.

6. Run the IDE on the board again.

Invalid Device Signature

Invalid device signature tends to pop up when the board selected on the IDE is different from the Arduino board in use, since each board would have its device signature. The solution to this issue is straightforward—all the user has to do is select the right board on the Arduino IDE. Should the problem persist, the user should flash the board with the most recent Arduino bootloader. This Arduino bootloader is available for download on the official website of Arduino.

Launch4j Error

The Launch4j error occurs when the Arduino IDE takes more time to come up, and you try to click a button. Launch4j is a Java tool used to make Java applications, like the Arduino IDE, to run as a regular Windows program. The error is bound to pop up when the Arduino IDE library is not compatible with the Java Runtime Environment (JRE). Just turn off the Bluetooth or WiFi connectivity of your computer to clear this error temporarily. A permanent solution is possible when you get the JRE in the IDE replaced with the latest version. Get a recent IDE downloaded and installed to address this issue.

Serial Port Already in Use

Interactions between the computer and other devices run through the serial port. So, users must first consider the action being executed by the serial port before they ask it to initiate different actions. Overburdening the serial data with multiple tasks at the same time tends to result in issues. The serial port already in use is a simple troubleshooting issue that you must resolve in no distant time. Do not use the serial port to do two things at a time; avoid launching the serial port when the board is using it to communicate with another device or software. Refrain from uploading a code that is currently in use. Close all software and tools that might be using the serial port or reset the Arduino board before you upload your code.

Uploads Successful but No Effect

If the Arduino IDE says the sketch is uploaded, but the board fails to do the needful, the user will have another troubleshooting issue. Resolve this with the following steps.

1. Be sure the target board is not different from the one selected in the Arduino IDE

2. Check whether the sketch size is within the capacity of the board

3. Adjust the power supply and make it stable.

Sketch Too Large

If the flash memory of the board is smaller than the size of the sketch, this troubleshooting problem will pop up. For example, this warning will pop up when one tries to upload a plan that is above 32KB on the Arduino Uno. This board comes with a 32KB flash memory, out of which 2KB has gone for the Arduino bootloader. Since the size of the sketch causes the problem, find a way to reduce the amount of space the plan currently occupies. Use the tips below to address the issue.

1. Consider using integer data types instead of afloat.

2. Use the "cost" qualifier to declare your variables.

3. Always go for lightweight versions of essential libraries.

4. Develop algorithms that support lightweight codes.

Consider moving the project to another board if the steps above do not yield the desired result. Arduino Mega is excellent for large projects, since its flash memory is enormous.

Java.lang.StackOverflow

Codes are commands that the board interprets to execute desired actions. When these codes are not encoded correctly, the board will have issues decoding them, hence this troubleshooting problem. The Arduino board uses certain expressions to process the sketch but may run into problems when it encounters typos, missing quotes, and other code errors in the plan. Such errors are the genesis of this troubleshooting problem. The project should get particular attention to identify these errors and correct them.

Missing Libraries or Header Files

Codes copied from online sources or tutorials may be hard to use for Arduino projects unless the right libraries run on the Arduino IDE. Trying to use such systems will subject such users to an error message, indicating that library or header files are missing. This troubleshooting issue can be resolved when the missing libraries or header files are installed. Use the Library Manager to search for the missing library or simply locate the required library online.

Final Words

Thank you for purchasing this book on Arduino Programming. Yes, some of the technical data may be a little confusing to begin with but follow the coding processes and you will achieve what you're after.

Be sure to purchase a hard copy if you only bought the kindle copy. We wish you well in your endeavours and ensure you have a greater understanding of what Arduino is and how it works.

Keep this book handy whilst you are programming, it will be a useful handbook.

Please leave a positive review as this will help others to learn how to use Arduino. The more people that use this method of programming the better it becomes for you, as you will have a new point of discussion with your friends.

Image Credits: Shutterstock.com

www.ingramcontent.com/pod-product-compliance
Lightning Source LLC
Chambersburg PA
CBHW070424220526
45466CB00004B/1533